P9-BYS-741

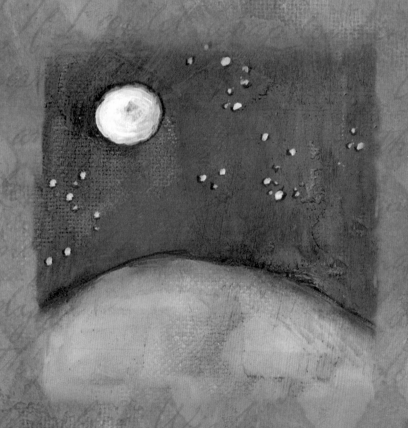

the dance. I wish you Love to hold when
it took to get there was a smile bursting with
the beginning of every dream. While we wa
to fragrance, then softly sings the lyrics to t
the stars at night. Wishing you a time of t
ries forever. If I could wrap love in a ribb
fanfare. I wish you a magical day. All the
d to look for and find. So come with me as
step we take through the valleys and the
that will never change, and the man in the
their melody plays hide and seek with th
with passing wisps of wisdom from
to the skies. Wishing you all the t
that sails through our day and our night
the dance. I wish you Love to hold when
it took to get there was a smile bursting with

ISBN 0-7683-2061-5

Text by Flavia and Lisa Weedn

Illustrations by Flavia Weedn

© Weedn Family Trust

www.flavia.com

All rights reserved.

Published in 1999 by Cedco Publishing Company

100 Pelican Way, San Rafael, California 94901

For a free catalog of other Cedco® products, please write

to the address above, or visit our website: www.cedco.com

Printed in Hong Kong

The artwork for each picture is digitally mastered using acrylic on canvas.

With love and gratitude to those kindred spirits whose dedication, endless support, and talented
hands made this book a reality – Lisa Mansfield, Jane Durand, Diana Musacchio, Tyler Tomblin,
Jennie Sparrow, Solveig Chandler, Hui-Ying Ting-Bornfreund, Kim Gendreau and Annette Berlin.

If I could sit across the porch from God,

I'd thank Him for this sweet life.

This is my journal of gratitude.

_____

(written by)

_____

(date)

A GRATITUDE JOURNAL

Across the Porch from God

Flavia and Lisa Weedn
Illustrated by Flavia Weedn

Cedco Publishing Company • San Rafael, California

When I was a child, I talked to the moon.

I thought God sat on the other side and patiently listened to my

thoughts, my hurts, my dreams. Although I'm a child no longer,

I still talk to the moon and I still believe God is listening. He's

right there on the porch of understanding, and I find there are

times I need him now more than I ever did before.

Life is the journey we all share. We love, feel, cry, care and

believe. We do the laundry and soothe a child's tears. We work until

we drop and then search for our romantic heart. We yearn to

become more and to help others, as we strive to make a difference,

however grand or small. Sometimes, in the whirlwind pursuit of

our days, we may be so busy looking ahead that we forget

to look up. Life's simple beauty may elude us,

yet this, too, is a part of the journey.

To reawaken our souls,

we need only open the window

and let the light in.

Divine miracles occur when we

remember to look upon our ordinary

moments as reverently as our extraordinary ones, and when we pause

to give thanks for having been given the blessed opportunity

to love, to dream, and to be.

These pages are more than a gratitude journal, more than a leap of faith.

They are designed to be your window to understanding.

It's safe here. So come, sit across the porch from God, open your heart

and let the miracle unfold.

Flavia

Table of Contents

Through My Window

In the Company of Angels

Sacred Moments

Unexpected Miracles

Finding Beauty • In the Ordinary

Discovering the Gift • Of the Human Spirit

Accepting the Grace • Of Small Miracles

Seeing New Landscapes • Of Nature's Wonder

The Path of Prayer • Reasons to Believe

Divine Revelations • Gazing Upward

Gifts of Grace

This Sweet Life • Sharing the Wonder

Gestures of Care • Making a Difference

Feeling Connected • Unconditional Love

Living with Purpose • Compassionate Soul

Making Peace • The Gift of Time

Understanding More • Gazing Upward

Giving Thanks & Praise

Through New Eyes • Impassioned Soul

Heaven and Earth • The Garden of Life

From the Heart • With More to Give

Taking the Time • Creating the Miracle

A Work in Progress • Embracing the Gift

Feeling More • Gazing Upward

*T*hrough my

WINDOW

I see the **reflection**

of my world. It can be

complicated and chaotic,

or peaceful and serene.

But BEAUTY is always

here, when I see through

the eyes of my H E A R T.

Through my Window

A View of My World

What I see in my everyday life . . .

- My family
  - - Ben playing with legos, singing
  - - Levi drawing and playing video games

the boys fighting

- Mom working, working, relaxing, and having self-contro

What Defines Me

How I view the person I am . . .

Just
to be
alive
and
aware
and
thankful
is
miracle
enough.

All That I Believe

God's touch upon my life and what I hold sacred . . .

Living My Faith

My convictions and how I act upon my beliefs . . . .

Soulful Passions

What moves and inspires me . . .

_____
_____
_____
_____
_____
_____
_____
_____
_____
_____
_____
_____
_____
_____
_____
_____

My Heart's Joy

What makes me happy . . .

Every heart has its passion. Doing what you love gives your spirit wings.

What Matters Most

Defining my priorities and letting go of the rest . . .

_____
_____
_____
_____
_____
_____
_____
_____
_____
_____
_____
_____
_____
_____
_____
_____
_____

Richness of Heart

Recognizing the miracles that surround me . . .

Defining My Truth

Exploring the voice of my heart . . .

_____

_____

_____

_____

_____

_____

_____

_____

_____

_____

_____

_____

_____

_____

_____

_____

_____

The Masquerade

Putting away the masks of illusion I sometimes wear . . .

Remember

who

you are.

Truth

is the

language

of heaven.

Becoming More

What I'd like to change and how I'd like to grow . . .

_____

_____

_____

_____

_____

_____

_____

_____

_____

_____

_____

_____

_____

_____

_____

Gazing Upward

Today I give thanks for . . .

*L*ife's

moments

are woven into

songs

and *silences*

only the **heart**

can hear.

Blessings of Solitude

Quiet times of reflection . . .

_____
_____
_____
_____
_____
_____
_____
_____
_____
_____
_____
_____
_____
_____
_____
_____
_____
_____

Finding Peace

Listening to my heart . . .

The human spirit needs a private place to dwell — a sanctuary of peace and inspiration.

Opening Windows

If I had the time, I would . . .

_____

_____

_____

_____

_____

_____

_____

_____

_____

_____

_____

_____

_____

_____

_____

_____

Unlocking Doors

What holds me back . . . .

_____

_____

_____

_____

_____

_____

_____

_____

_____

_____

_____

_____

_____

_____

_____

_____

Truthful Awakenings

The hardest questions to ask . . .

Soulful Discoveries

The answers I seek, I already own . . .

Hope is the song we sing to ourselves. It may be difficult to hear sometimes, but it is always there, deep within our hearts.

Leaps of Faith

Letting faith conquer fear . . .

Heeding the Spirit

When love, hope and trust lead the way . . .

_____

_____

_____

_____

_____

_____

_____

_____

_____

_____

_____

_____

_____

_____

_____

_____

Lessons of Abundance

Being thankful for what we have makes room for more . . .

_____

_____

_____

_____

_____

_____

_____

_____

_____

_____

_____

_____

_____

_____

_____

_____

_____

Treasures Untold

The wisdom of the heart . . .

Life is the gift and time is the treasure. Listen to your heart, for it is wiser than you know.

Moving Forward

Promises I make to myself . . .

Gazing Upward

Today I give thanks for . . .

_____

_____

_____

_____

_____

_____

_____

_____

_____

_____

_____

_____

_____

_____

Angels are

all **around** us,

and any H E A R T

that *yearns* to

can reach out

and **touch**

a wing.

In the Company of Angels

Family and Friends

Those who share my world . . .

_____
_____
_____
_____
_____
_____
_____
_____
_____
_____
_____
_____
_____
_____
_____
_____

Treasured Hearts

The love and joy they bring me . . .

If
I could
sit across
the porch
from God,
I'd thank
Him for
lending
me you.

Circle of Touch

Hands I hold . . .

Blanket of Comfort

The gift of caring hearts . . .

Cherished Memories

Pieces in time my heart has saved . . .

_____

_____

_____

_____

_____

_____

_____

_____

_____

_____

_____

_____

_____

_____

_____

_____

_____

_____

Tapestries of the Heart

How others have helped me become the person I am . . .

That which the heart has cherished becomes a part of us forever.

Angels Among Us

Moments of connection that have changed my world . . .

Of Grace and Kindness

The beauty of the human spirit . . .

There Are No Strangers

People I'd like to know . . .

In the Presence of Care

All that I'd like to share . . .

That

we

could

live

our lives

at the

same time

on earth,

how

incredible

God's

plan.

Learning through Love

What I hope to give back for all that I've been given . . .

_____

_____

_____

_____

_____

_____

_____

_____

_____

_____

_____

_____

_____

_____

_____

_____

_____

_____

Gazing Upward

Today I give thanks for . . .

*B*elieve

in your HEART

that something

wonderful is

about to happen.

Unexpected Miracles

Finding Beauty

Opening my eyes to more . . .

_____

_____

_____

_____

_____

_____

_____

_____

_____

_____

_____

_____

_____

_____

_____

_____

_____

_____

In the Ordinary

Life's simple blessings . . .

We are unaware of what sweet miracles may come.

Discovering the Gift

Feeling connected . . .

Of the Human Spirit

Surrounded by love . . .

_____

_____

_____

_____

_____

_____

_____

_____

_____

_____

_____

_____

_____

_____

_____

Accepting the Grace

Learning to receive . . .

_____

_____

_____

_____

_____

_____

_____

_____

_____

_____

_____

_____

_____

_____

_____

_____

_____

_____

_____

Of Small Miracles

Embracing each moment . . .

It is

in the

small

things

that the

spirit is

touched

and feels

great

joy.

Seeing New Landscapes

Recognizing the beauty of God's world . . .

_____

_____

_____

_____

_____

_____

_____

_____

_____

_____

_____

_____

_____

_____

_____

_____

_____

Of Nature's Wonder

The incredibility of creation . . . .

The Path of Prayer

Private conversations with God . . .

_____

_____

_____

_____

_____

_____

_____

_____

_____

_____

_____

_____

_____

_____

_____

_____

Reasons to Believe

Finding clarity and direction through gratitude . . .

Heaven

smiles

softly

and

hears

every

wish.

Divine Revelations

Opening my heart and becoming more . . .

Gazing Upward

Today I give thanks for . . .

_____

_____

_____

_____

_____

_____

_____

_____

_____

_____

_____

_____

_____

_____

_____

We are

each a part of

one another.

Care is the

golden thread

that connects

us all.

Gifts of Grace

This Sweet Life

Beholding the miracle . . .

_____
_____
_____
_____
_____
_____
_____
_____
_____
_____
_____
_____
_____
_____
_____
_____
_____
_____
_____
_____

Sharing the Wonder

What I hope to pass along to others . . .

Some people leave footprints on our hearts, and we are never, ever the same.

Gestures of Care

Daily offerings of kindness . . .

Making a Difference

Extending my hand and heart . . .

Feeling Connected

Embracing the common link we all share . . .

_____

_____

_____

_____

_____

_____

_____

_____

_____

_____

_____

_____

_____

_____

_____

_____

Unconditional Love

Growing through acceptance and forgiveness . . .

There
is no
greater
wisdom
than
kindness.

Living with Purpose

Finding my place in the world . . .

_____
_____
_____
_____
_____
_____
_____
_____
_____
_____
_____
_____
_____
_____
_____
_____
_____
_____
_____

Compassionate Soul

Remembering what matters . . .

Making Peace

Creating my sanctuary . . .

The Gift of Time

Embrace

each day

in the

spirit

of joy,

for life is

brief and all

too fragile

to let it

go by in

haste.

Understanding More

Lessons I'm learning . . .

_____

_____

_____

_____

_____

_____

_____

_____

_____

_____

_____

_____

_____

_____

_____

Gazing Upward

Today I give thanks for . . .

Honoring

life's **miracle**

is a **gift** we give

to God, and

every **whisper**

of thanks

is a **song** we

sing for Him.

Giving
Thanks
&
Praise

Through New Eyes

Seeing more than before . . .

_____

_____

_____

_____

_____

_____

_____

_____

_____

_____

_____

_____

_____

Impassioned Soul

Feeling the abundance . . .

We
plant
seeds of
hope
and then
one
morning
we wake
to see a
field of
mira-
cles.

Heaven and Earth

In awe of the world I live in . . .

The Garden of Life

The ever-present wonder . . .

_____

_____

_____

_____

_____

_____

_____

_____

_____

_____

_____

_____

_____

_____

_____

_____

From the Heart

Understanding there are no limits to love . . .

_____

_____

_____

_____

_____

_____

_____

_____

_____

_____

_____

_____

_____

_____

_____

With More to Give

Discovering new strengths within me . . .

Strength

is born

of love,

and

nothing is

impossible

to the

believing

heart.

Taking the Time

Welcoming change . . .

Creating the Miracle

Letting the beauty unfold . . .

_____
_____
_____
_____
_____
_____
_____
_____
_____
_____
_____
_____
_____
_____
_____
_____
_____
_____
_____
_____

A Work in Progress

Following my heart . . .

_____

_____

_____

_____

_____

_____

_____

_____

_____

_____

_____

_____

_____

_____

_____

_____

_____

_____

Embracing the Gift

Living with passion . . .

Be

not

forgetful

to celebrate

being

alive.

Feeling More

All that I am grateful for . . .

Gazing Upward

Giving thanks and praise . . .

Flavia

Photos by Chris Chandler

Lisa and her daughter Sylvie

Flavia Weedn is one of America's leading contemporary inspirational writers and illustrators. Offering hope for the human spirit, Flavia portrays the basic excitement, simplicity and beauty she sees in the ordinary things of life. Her work has touched the lives of millions for over three decades.

Lisa Weedn, Flavia's daughter and co-author, shares her mother's philosophy and passion. For over fifteen years, Lisa's writings have been a quiet messenger of the fundamental truth that age has no barrier on feelings of the human heart.

Their collaborative work, which celebrates life and embraces meaningful core values, can be found in numerous books, collections of fine stationery goods, giftware, and lifestyle products distributed worldwide.

Flavia and Lisa live in Santa Barbara, California.

different to each of us, but how
moments of
on earth
buried so deep
together and our
flowers grow freely. There
Days sing their
to me, and you awake
on the wings of
all things good and wonderful
life is different to each of us, but how